Dear Mrs. Simon,
    This seemed an appropriate book for someone whose day is surrounded with "Children's Voices"!
    Thank you for the loving environment you've created for Joshua. We appreciate all your efforts and the special part you are providing in Josh's educational foundation.
        Merry Christmas!
        Dave & Nannette Hansen

JoshuaH.

Children's Voices

Children's Voices

Clifton H. Jolley

Bookcraft
Salt Lake City, Utah

Library of Congress Catalog Card Number: 84-70990

ISBN 0-88494-532-4

First Printing, 1984

Lithographed in the United States of America
PUBLISHERS PRESS
Salt Lake City, Utah

For Mother
who gave me voice
and
for Marcia
whose voice teaches me to listen
to the smaller voices we have made

Contents

Rachel

Calvin

Preface

When I began collecting these small essays to be published as a book, I immediately began to categorize them: three seemed to be about fear; two were about death; some were humorous, some not.

It was a tidy way to organize, but it had nothing to do with the essays themselves. The essays never were designed to teach, or to prove, or to do anything more than record—record the voices of five children and the resonance of those voices in my life.

What those voices have to say did not come neatly filed and cross-referenced; it just came . . . from Calvin, Rachel, Sarah, Aaron, and Patricia—five children who are more like other children than they are remarkable. And as you read what they have said, you inevitably will think, "My children say things like that, only more witty, more profound, more essentially true."

And you will be right. Because the children's voices that we hear ring more brilliantly than the ones we must imagine from essays designed to capture them.

The problem is that we do not listen as carefully as we should, or that we try to make more of those small voices than the pleasure they are. What children say is important not because it is wise (although frequently it is wise), but because it is true in ways in which only children are true —not intellectually or even morally, but viscerally. Children *live* the truth—in their enthusiasm, their simplicity, their earnestness; even in their anger and their fear. They apprehend the world uniquely, and they define it with a sympathetic language that is itself a joyful endorsement of life.

Which is why I wrote these essays: so as not to forget the moments when the world spun through each of my children like white light through a prism. I fail to catch all the refractions of those moments, but perhaps I catch enough of them for you to hear the voices I have heard, for you to recognize and appreciate voices of your own.

All of these essays have appeared in my "Voices" column in the *Deseret News,* with the exception of "A Child's Worth," which was published in the *New York Times* in February 1979.

Patricia

A Gifted Elbow

"My elbow sings," Patricia said.

Marcia was clearing the table, filling the dishwasher, distracted. "You mean it *stings*," she replied, correcting Patricia's pronunciation.

"No, it doesn't hurt. It *sings*. A little."

Marcia stopped, laid on the counter the bunch of knives and forks she was about to manage into the dishwasher, and looked at Patricia. "It sings?"

"Yes."

Patricia is the youngest of our five children, and Marcia does not argue with her. Marcia does not argue with Patricia, because Patricia is beautiful (the first of our children not to look like a frog for six months after she was born), Patricia is spoiled (her four brothers and sisters protect her as though she were the last of the blood royal), and Marcia has grown wise. The four children before Patricia have taught Marcia how futile is any effort to overcome a child's logic. Futile, and maybe wrong.

"What does your elbow sing?"

"Oh, just little songs. It sings these little songs to me."

"Really? When?"

"When I sing. It needs a little help, so it sings along with me. I'm not singing right now, that's why you can't hear it."

How very nice to have an elbow that sings. Marcia and I should have taught all our children the necessity of it. But lacking the advantage of parental instruction, Patricia had gone out and discovered it for herself: a singing elbow can keep you company when your brothers and sisters are at school, can cheer a day made lonely by your *onlyness;* a singing elbow can remind you how the tune goes.

Even if adults might not agree that there are advantages in an elbow that sings, certainly there are none who would contend that there are *disadvantages.* Patricia's elbow performs all the normal functions: bends her arm through the middle, rests on tables while she eats, serves as a platform for her cupped hand to cradle her chin against, wears through sweaters at the sleeve—the whole job description. It's just that it does this other thing, too.

And why not? Why not in a world where people look, eat, dress, and *work* the same way—why not have one person who works a little differently? Why not let there be at least one person, however small, whose elbow sings.

"Do you think you could get your elbow to sing a little song for me?" Marcia asked.

"No, not really. It's tired. And a little shy. It only sings when it's alone."

"But *you're* there when it sings."

"Yes, but that's OK, 'cause I'm that way too."

That way. Whatever *way* it is that makes her elbow sing—that *allows* her elbow to sing—Patricia is *that way,* too. And maybe that explains what is wrong with the rest of us. We aren't enough *that way.*

And perhaps the world is so sorry a place because there are so few of us who are. If only there were more of us who had Patricia's gift; then—when life got tense, when we were afraid—instead of lashing out, we could lean to a friend and ask, "You want to hear my elbow sing?" And perhaps the friend would answer, "Sure. In fact, if yours knows the tune, mine will sing harmony."

"My elbow doesn't sing, you know," Marcia told Patricia.

"No," Patricia agreed, "it doesn't."

Tied Up in Toes

If you want Patricia to stay awake for an extra twenty minutes to see her grandmother who has just flown in from California, she will be nodding and groggy a full half hour before bedtime. But if you want her to get to sleep on time so as to be ready for a family outing on the next day, you will hear her giggling softly in her room long past midnight.

No matter. This is the order of the universe. If children were no trouble to put to bed, there would be no reason for parents.

So, when Marcia passed Patricia's room and saw her lying on her bed playing with her toes, Marcia was not upset. But she did want quiet.

"Patricia, stop playing with your toes and go to sleep."

"I'm not playing!" Patricia protested, in that tone of indignant righteousness that creeps into her voice when she is more certain than sorry.

"Patricia, I saw you playing with your toes. I'm not angry, but you must stop it and go to sleep."

"I told you, I'm not playing with them! I'm untying them!"

Toes that tie. I think I like that nearly as much as an elbow that sings.

"You were what?" Marcia asked, certain she had misunderstood.

"They're tangled. Crooked and tangled. Like my hair. Only it's my toes. I'm getting them loose."

There is no explaining to Patricia that toes are unlike hair, that they do not snarl. And no reason. There is no reason for a child's perception of disorder to be less valuable and valued than more mature, less original observations.

"Well, I'm sorry I made a mistake," Marcia apologized, trying not to smile, "but I think you've had time enough to get the toes straightened out. So, turn over and go to sleep."

Patricia did not turn over. Not right away. She raised herself on one elbow, the embers of her indignity now fanned to full burning, and she tremblingly said, "You don't care! You don't even care that my toes are all mixed up. So I'm just going to leave them, and that's the way they'll be." And she flung herself against the wall, where she sobbed a few minutes into the wallpaper and then went to sleep.

We live in a world beyond our knowing, full of stupefying complications. There are explanations, but probably not the explanations we make. We make the wrong connections, infer the wrong emphases. Simply: we misunderstand.

Since Marcia told me about Patricia's toes, I have been haunted by an image. It is the vision of a young lady; a beautiful young lady, except for her feet. Her feet are like baseballs, the toes grown over and around themselves, knotted beyond any hope of undoing them.

"There was a time when I might have set things right," she is saying to all who will listen, "but I was not allowed."

And people look at her feet, and shake their heads, and say to one another, "Who would have believed such a thing?"

Patricia: I believe. And your mother more than I. We believe that the world can tangle toes, and other things. And we know how much time and work it takes to straighten them. Time, and work, and help.

You have always cried when your mother brushed through your snarled hair, and there is no comb to pull the tangles out of toes. Perhaps there are knots that must be worked alone to be undone, and knottings only a child can see . . . at night . . . in the solemn loneliness of bed too early and sleep too late.

Patricia and Sebastian

Patricia spends too much time talking to Sebastian, our dog.

I should be pleased Patricia is becoming such an amiable conversationalist, and I should let her speak with whomever she chooses. But having a daughter who prefers to chat with the family mutt rather than with me is . . . disconcerting.

It started after Sebastian's stay with my brother, Vernon. We were going to spend some time in Hawaii, and dogs being taken into that state (where there is no rabies) are subject to a six-month quarantine. Since we weren't planning on staying much longer than that, and since we thought quarantine would be cruel for Sebastian (and expensive for us), we decided not to take him.

Instead, we arranged for him to stay at Vernon's. Vernon lives on a three-acre ranch in Southern California where he raises goats and dogs and children. We thought it would be a pleasant place for Sebastian to spend a few months. But we didn't take into account the complications of burrs and coyotes.

Schnauzers have a wiry coat that irreversibly tangles with foxtails and weeds. If the tangles aren't groomed out, they stay. And they work their way in to bury in the animal's flesh, where they fester and produce open wounds.

Vernon is not much given to the bourgeois grooming of pets; what the beast doesn't do for itself doesn't get done. Maybe that's the way it should be, but it means schnauzers are in for a lot of grief at Vernon's.

After six months of burrs and matting, Sebastian was in pretty bad shape. Then, a week before we picked him up, he tangled with a coyote. There's nothing puny about a schnauzer, except its size. But Sebastian is too civilized a creature to do very well against a wild dog. So by the time we picked Sebastian up . . . I thought we might have to have him "put to sleep."

It was about that time that he and Patricia began having their chats. Under any circumstance Sebastian is a good listener; he does not interrupt. But after we picked him up—so near death the vet was uncertain he would last the night—he was even more attentive. He lay in the box we prepared with bath towels for his bed, his head lying over the cardboard edge and resting on Patricia's lap, his eyes usually closed but occasionally opening briefly to look up at Patricia, who went on and on, speaking of this and that.

Patricia sat with Sebastian through most of that first day when we brought Sebastian home. And when it was time for her to go to bed, she insisted that his bed be moved next to hers. As I turned out the light, I saw her hand go out to him. As I closed the door, I heard the conversation begin again.

And Sebastian, whom the vet had not thought would live, lived.

After he was well, whenever Patricia would call, he would go to her, lay his head again in her lap, and listen. Or sometimes they would just sit, Patricia idly fingering his moustache and eyebrows.

Patricia used to sit on my lap and finger *my* eyebrows. Of course, I paid less attention to her than Sebastian does. I was always a little distracted. Sebastian understands better the importance of what Patricia says.

A schnauzer may always be relied on to give you his complete attention. Especially if you are prepared to stroke his moustache and sing him songs . . . and sit by him until he heals. So Sebastian and Patricia have formed a fast friendship, because they were there for one another.

I had not thought it possible to envy a dog. Especially not Sebastian, who limps and is scarred. But I envy him. I envy Patricia's attention to him, her conversations with him and stroking of his hair.

And I envy his good sense, his attention to her, his instincts that communicate the final truth: that there is nothing so important, that will last so long or mean so much, as a little girl's conversation, as Patricia's love.

Sand Dunes, Sinkholes, Coyotes, and the Dark

You can take Highway 68 out of Lehi, Utah, go south around the west shore of Utah Lake to Elberta, then west on Highway 6, up the grade to Eureka, past Silver City, to the Little Sahara Sand Dunes.

But the easier route is straight south on I-15 to Nephi, then west on Highway 132. It's longer, but you avoid the grade. You also miss Eureka. I-15 is the way most people go, because they're pulling trailers heavy with three wheelers and dune buggies, and missing Eureka isn't missing much.

There are varieties of sage that grow only at the edge of the dunes of the Little Sahara. And there are coyotes that make their burrows there, and rustle through the tall brush at night, calling to one another across the bone-white sand, and crying at the white moon.

We sat around a fire late that night, the air finally free of the noise and exhaust of the dune buggies trying for the top of Sand Mountain. And the calling of the coyotes came up clear and startling against the horizon.

It was the first time my children (raised in cities) had heard the sound, and even the older children were uneasy. The youngest were terrified.

Patricia ran to me from the other side of the fire pit, climbed into my lap, and whispered, "The noise. . . . That noise. . . . It troubles me a little."

Patricia always talks in a euphemistic maturity that is a laughable paradox to her seven-year-old frame. She was not merely "troubled"; she was afraid.

"There's nothing to be afraid of," a friend who was camping with us told the children. "They're more afraid of you than you are of them. Coyotes live in holes in the ground, they're so afraid."

Patricia clutched at me and was not comforted; she knew that it was not possible for anything to be more frightened than she was. She knew that coyotes had nearly killed her dog, Sebastian. And she knew that anything that lives in a hole is more fearsome than fearful.

"Besides, a coyote isn't very big; just a small dog; coyotes can't kill anything bigger than a rabbit or a lamb."

Patricia isn't any bigger than a lamb, and she held onto me all the tighter. Late that night when it was time to go to bed, she would not go. For the first time in her life, she knew what lives in the night, knew the sound it makes; and she was afraid.

The next day the children played in the sand and scouted through the hills and gullies. The older children came back from one expedition shouting, "We found them; we found the tracks the coyotes made; they're real close; come see."

Patricia did not want to see.

Patricia had seen what coyotes had done to Sebastian —she had touched the festering wound behind his left leg and had felt him lean away from her; she had seen the patches where the wild dogs had bitten away Sebastian's gray fur, exposing his gray flesh and (where the flesh was torn) the pink meat of his muscle above his left shoulder bone.

Patricia did not want to see the *other* tracks the coyotes made.

That afternoon I decided to take the shorter, less-traveled way home, through Eureka. In the early evening, before the coyotes came again from their burrows, we packed the car and headed North on Highway 6.

I pulled off the road at Silver City and pointed out the rusting mine machinery and fallen-in mining shacks, then stopped again on the outskirts of Eureka to see the sinkhole that is supposed to have a house at the bottom of it. The land around Eureka has collapsed in several places from the careless shoring of the mine shafts. They say the big hole south of town opened up and swallowed the house only moments after its occupants tumbled out of the back door onto solid ground.

Patricia held with white fingers to the wire fence that keeps sightseers away, and she tried to see over the edge and into the hole. She didn't say anything.

As we walked back to the car, she held my hand and watched her feet as she kicked at rocks beside the highway, and finally asked, "Is that hole where the devil lives?"

I told her no, although it occurred to me later that it wasn't a bad image for hell—a deep pit wired about to keep people from falling in, but people forever curious about it, forever looking into it, forever imagining the bottom.

But I didn't want to confuse her with metaphor and metaphysics; I told her no; I told her it was just a hole.

"Oh," she said, "like the coyotes live in."

And I could tell that for her there is no difference between them—between this hole, the coyotes' burrows, and hell.

All are frightening. All are real.

There are other ways to get to the desert. But go through Eureka; stop at the rusted posts and wire outside of town; then go on to the dunes, and at night listen for the coyotes. You'll learn what I have learned: Patricia is right.

The Position Papers
of Childhood

Patricia has been sending me letters. Seven-year-old letters.

I find them taped to my word processor, tucked beneath my pillow, pushed under my bedroom and office doors.

Everyone in the family has been getting them, each note printed on the Garfield stationery she received for Christmas—a fat, orange, black-striped cat sitting on the lower right corner of each page. The cat is smiling.

The notes all begin the same: "I love you. . . ." The notes all end the same: "Love, Tricia." And in between, although the language of each is unique, the purpose of each is the same.

To Aaron, who is two years older and the most frequent conflict in her life, she wrote: "I love you, even when you don't let me sleep in your room. Love, Tricia." Patricia likes to sleep in Aaron's room because there is no place for Patricia to sleep but on the floor. The floor is bigger than her bed and does not need to be made. Usually Aaron likes having Patricia sleep on his floor, but occasionally he says no . . . so that Patricia will know whose floor it is.

And occasionally Marcia says no to Patricia's frequent requests to sleep on the floor. During the winter the floor is too cold. And during any season, the probability that Aaron and Patricia will lie awake playing—him handing toys down to her; the toys he keeps tucked under his covers until we turn out the light—the probability of such diversion from sleep is great. To Marcia Patricia wrote: "I love you, even when you are mad at me. Love, Tricia."

Years from now in an archival search, Patricia's letters will be discovered by a young and eager historian who will write a monograph concerning the enormous charity of a child capable of returning good for evil, tenderness for wrath, love for the constant anger of a mother too insensitive with rage to be moved by the tenderness of a child. Marcia is almost never angry with Patricia. But just before the letter came, she had told Patricia she couldn't sleep on Aaron's floor.

Calvin's letter said: "I love you, even when you yell at me. Love, Tricia." Calvin is Patricia's oldest brother. And to be fair, he yells a bit. Being the oldest is not easy; there are so many younger people to annoy you. So, Calvin does raise his voice, but virtually never at his youngest sister, Patricia.

To Sarah Patricia wrote: "I love you, even when you won't talk to me. Love, Tricia." Sarah will talk to virtually anyone, whether her conversation is wanted or not. But the day before the letter came, Sarah had been busy playing with her friends. Too busy to answer Patricia's question about a bug she found crawling on the floor in Aaron's room.

Rachel received a letter which said: "I love you, even when you bug me. Love, Tricia." Patricia is easily "bugged." It is her most recent explanation for why she does not wish to sit next to so-and-so, for why she is behaving in thus-and-such a way. Patricia is discovering a world in which most things "bug" her at one time or another. She is discovering a world like the one we have known.

Each of her letters reaches out to that world, commenting on it, defining it by the power of her seven-year-old vision; not so much accepting it as wanting it to change, and finding in the language of acceptance and love a vehicle for change. Patricia is writing not merely letters but position papers, manifestos of the revolution she intends, of the brave new world in which she will sleep on whichever floors she chooses, speak to whomever she pleases, and be the center of a universe which is never angry or inclined to bug.

Yesterday, I received a letter from Patricia. "I love you, even when you are nuts, I still love you. Love, Tricia."

Likewise.

Things That Are Fun Only When You Do Them Together

I had taken Patricia for the morning so that Marcia could keep an appointment to play racquetball.

"I don't have to go," Marcia told me, "but the racquetball game is at eleven-thirty, and Patricia has to be at school by twelve. If you're busy, I'll cancel the game."

I was busy. I'm always busy these days. But Marcia doesn't ask frequently, and on the spur of the moment I simply couldn't think of any reason why getting Patricia to school should be more Marcia's than my responsibility.

"She'll have to go to the office with me, but sure. . . ."

I even helped get Patricia dressed. Everything but her hair. (A little girl's hair looks worse *after* I've combed it.) But I helped pick out her clothes, and pull on her socks, and lace her shoes. I did any number of things of which Patricia told me, "I can do that myself, Daddy."

Since when? I can distinctly remember doing *all* these things for *all* my children since . . . since forever! Not recently, perhaps. I've been busy just recently . . .

"I've put on my own shoes and socks since before I started kindergarten. Mommy taught me."

And about time, too. Can't go on dressing children forever, can you?

Still, it would have been nice to notice the learning. Nice to watch her pull on that first sock and clumsily lace her shoe. And as she pulled on her coat, I wondered what I had been busy with while she was busy with learning to do these things I used to do for her.

As we drove to the office, I told Patricia, "I'll get you some paper and pencils so you can draw." She smiled and slid a little closer to me on the front seat. Blonde. And not quite tall enough to see over the dash. But taller than I remembered. She had been only four pounds eleven ounces when she was born, and she was jaundiced. We worried about her a lot the first few months. I remember holding her for hours at a time, looking at her tiny yellow hands, at the nearly microscopic nail on each miniature finger.

"There's lots of paper at my office," I said to make conversation. Patricia went on smiling.

The work I had to do took longer than I'd planned. Trouble resolving the transition in a document. Transitions frequently are difficult. You lose track of them. You think you have control of the words and the spaces between, only to discover you missed something, that something doesn't make sense. You have to pay attention all the time, or the moment and the movement get away from you.

But Patricia lay beside my desk on her stomach and drew, only interrupting me once. She scratched on the underside of her arm where a fly had landed, looked at the delicate red etchings where her fingernails had traced, and asked: "Daddy, why doesn't it tickle when you tickle yourself?"

"I don't know, dear. Daddy's busy right now."

By the time I finished the work, it was twelve-eighteen.

"We're late," Patricia said, not too young to be kind (*I* was late, and *she* was inconvenienced by it). But she was enjoying herself, in spite of my having ignored her. I looked at her—all pink, and blonde, and blue-eyed—and realized how much a literary convention she would be if I had created her in a story rather than in the flesh. No one would believe Patricia in a story, and it was difficult for me to believe her at that moment, or to remember when it was between the time she had been yellow and the time she turned so pink that I had seen her so closely as then, or now.

"Tell you what. Let's skip school. Let's you and me go out to lunch. And afterwards, we'll take care of some *business* at the mall, in a few toy stores. And maybe we'll be home in time for dinner, and maybe we won't."

And we did. And while she ate a sandwich, and while she looked at dolls, I looked at her small fingers, and her still-miniature nails.

And we did get home in time for dinner. Just. And surprisingly, Marcia (who is more responsible than I) was not upset that Patricia had missed school.

I passed Patricia's room that evening as Marcia tucked her into bed, and I stood in the hall and listened to Patricia tell her mother about the things she had done with her father. And as Marcia turned out the light, Patricia asked, "Mommy, why doesn't it tickle when you tickle yourself?"

"Because," Marcia replied, "there are some things that just aren't any fun unless you do them together."

Aaron

A Place to Go

Aaron is a perfectly good boy. But we worry.

Occasionally when I get home from work, I find his mother poking at her favorite Boston fern—a plant of once-enormous size which has been in a constant state of decline since we purchased it. Marcia only tends the fern when she needs a good worry; so if I find her at it, I ask what is wrong.

"It's dying."

"Yes, I know; but what else?"

"Nothing."

And we leave it at that. She pokes at the fern, I watch, and in a few minutes she will usually say, "We had better keep an eye on Aaron."

But Aaron requires almost no watching. Unlike our other children, who need only thirty seconds alone to consume half the contents of a medicine chest, Aaron is

obedient, trustworthy, and—the greatest blessing of all—
noninquisitive.

Some parents go on and on about the "active little
minds" of their children, but that is usually no more than an
excuse for the damage the little barbarians are likely to do to
your home. Give Aaron a game or toy in a room to himself
and he will not molest you or what belongs to you.

Which is not to say that his mind is not active. Aaron is
always thinking. It is simply impossible to get any notion
about what he is thinking.

So we worry. We have worried since he was three years
old and told us about his house.

While I was cooking vegetables in a newly acquired
microwave oven, Aaron sat and watched—curiously, I
might have thought, but with Aaron it is difficult to say. Just
as I was about to take out a bowl of steaming carrots,
Aaron, his eyes still fixed on the oven's black door, said, "I
have one of those at my house."

No stranger to the faulty syntax of a child, I responded,
"Yes, of course we have."

"No," he corrected me, "not here; at my other house.
At my house. At my very own house."

At first I thought he had been confused by our recent
move. But during the next several weeks I was to learn that
he was not thinking of a house I had any knowledge of,
except through him. It was white and large, and had a
green roof and a microwave oven.

It also had a changeable number of bedrooms. Occasionally, when he suggested we might visit him there, we
were told that we would all have to sleep in the same

room—on the floor, since there would be room in his bed only for Calvin, his older brother who had recently let him sleep on the top bunk with him. But another time, when Marcia said she wouldn't like sleeping together on the floor, he said there was enough room now—everyone would have their own bed, their own bedroom. Although that seemed an improvement, Marcia reminded him that a few days before he had had only one bedroom; how could there now be so many?

Less subtle minds, such as Marcia's and mine, are troubled by such inconsistencies; but Aaron, with that perfect clarity we have come to expect of him, was unperturbed. As he turned to run downstairs, he easily explained: "That's just how it is."

And it just may be. Of course, we were troubled at first, and now, years since we learned of his house, we still occasionally worry. But often I think how pleasant it must be to have a house of one's "very own"; a place that is white, with a green roof and a microwave oven; that has however many rooms one needs at any particular time. When Aaron is angry, or troubled, or afraid, his head goes down, his hands go into his pockets, and he mutters, "I'm gonna go to my house." Then he is off, out of the door and around the corner of our yard to where we cannot see.

Recently Marcia mentioned Aaron's "other" house to my father, who is a psychologist.

"What's it all about?" she asked.

"One of two things," he replied. "Either he's schizophrenic or he's normal."

It was not the sort of joke Marcia was prepared to find

funny, so he went on: "The important thing is that he wouldn't have built the house if he hadn't needed it."

Children have that sort of necessary wisdom: they are not afraid to give themselves what they need. Aaron needed the house. I don't know why. All I am certain of is that he did need it, that against all contrary evidence and logic he acquired it, and that it would have been a greater failure to deprive him of it than to have tried to understand his need.

And once I had overcome my adult rationality, the house was easy enough to understand: someplace to go when Aaron needed a few minutes to regroup, to gather his courage and energy about him; not so much an "escape" as a "retreat," for he always returned to us from it, and most of the time he actually preferred our company to his house's solitude. But on those occasions when there was simply more than he knew what to do with or how to handle—when we did not serve him as we should have, or appeared to be in league against him—he was out of the door and around the corner, and I knew where he was going.

Not so often by the time he turned four. He was growing up. Which had me worrying again. I had rather envied him his house, his place to go and enjoy a peace that was always of appropriate size and kind. I had even toyed with the idea of getting one of my own. Of course, I would have fashioned mine of more substantial stuff than a child's fantasy—cedar shake and timbers on the bank of a narrow stream where trout would rise to dry flies at dusk—but its purpose would have been the same: someplace to go.

So I mourned the passing of my child into a more sensible world where there is often no place to go, no help for pain, too many rooms or too few.

Then one afternoon, as I mowed my way around the yard, I found Aaron standing in the backyard, staring at the seven-thousand-foot mountain behind our house.

"I have one of those," he said.

And I knew that everything was going to be just fine.

Not Wanting to Be
As Wild As Patricia

"Understanding a person does not mean condoning; it only means that one does not accuse him as if one were God or a judge placed above him."
—Erich Fromm, *Man for Himself*

Aaron does not treat Patricia as though she were a seven-year-old servant to his nine-year-old needs. Not quite. But that's pretty much the way Patricia sees it.

Part of the problem is that they sleep in the same bedroom. When we first arrived at the arrangement, it seemed sensible enough. Rachel and Sarah in the attic bedroom, where they would have a bit of room to spread out. Calvin in the northwest bedroom, alone, because someone had to be alone, and he is thirteen. Patricia and Aaron in the northeast bedroom, because they were too young to be very choosey, and they were happy when we told them they should be happy to have any place at all.

But over the last several months, Aaron has begun to behave as though he is in training to become an Alabama chain gang boss bossing a gang of one.

"She bothers me," Aaron protests. And he's right. *Everything* Patricia does bothers Aaron. If she throws her clothes on the floor, it bothers him . . . because hers get mixed up with his. If she puts her clothes away, Aaron is bothered . . . because she puts them in the wrong drawer, or leaves the drawer ajar, or is "just trying to make me look bad."

Aaron is bothered not merely by what Patricia does, but by Patricia.

And at the same time, he is not. Much of the time they play very happily together. But the times Marcia and I are more likely to notice are the times when Aaron has just tempted Patricia to climb into a sleeping bag, and has pulled the draw string shut to hear her squeal.

"He should be me and me him for just a little while," Patricia recently sobbed to Marcia. "Then he would know how *wild* it is to be me."

It has never occurred to me that being Patricia might be "wild." It has never occurred to Aaron. Aaron and I don't think much at all about the way Patricia feels; we focus on when she squeals, to Aaron's delight and my concern. Most of the time Aaron and I respond only to the things about Patricia that bother us, telling her to do them differently, and ignoring her when she does.

Neither Aaron nor I have spent much time thinking about what Patricia feels. We have spent no more time thinking about what she *is*.

Several years ago when Marcia and I toured the Soviet

Union, we were startled to discover that *their* political literature describes *us* in the same terms *our* political literature describes *them*. It's tempting to say the difference is that *our* literature is true. But that is a simple temptation that reveals the Soviet system, but not its people. I've never tried to imagine how "wild" it must be to be a Russian, how a Russian feels, what a Russian *is*. My opinions are prejudiced rather than informed.

When I suggested Patricia's changing-places plan to Aaron, he replied, "I wouldn't want to be Patricia in a million years!"

And that's the trouble.

Being Afraid

"But you don't understand," Aaron said, his eyes bright as brown agate. "I'm a little bit afraid."

I did understand. When he was four, Aaron had not wanted us to leave him alone in Sunday School. Church may seem an unlikely place in which to be afraid, but Aaron was terrified. So, I relearned Bible stories while sitting with him on chairs too small for me. And I seduced him away from his fear, teaching him that there is nothing in church to be afraid of; teaching him that Jesus would keep him safe.

And one day, when I suggested he go to his class with his friends, he said "OK."

Aaron did not ask me to go with him again. And I was glad for him. But over the next several weeks at church, I missed his hand on my leg, his sitting close to me while we learned of the children of Israel delivered from Pharaoh, the babies of Bethlehem not delivered from Herod.

"I am a little bit afraid," he said, unwilling to go to bed alone; and I thought, *we have come through this before.*

I was wrong.

Nine-year-olds are leaner than four-year-olds. Less baby fat. Fewer baby fears.

"I'm not afraid of Draclea," he said, still unable to pronounce the Transylvanian count's name. "That kinda thing doesn't scare me, because it can't happen, y'know? What I think about when I try to go to sleep are beings and creatures from other planets."

Beings and creatures. From other planets. His exact words.

For this I might blame *Star Wars.* But all the movie did was provide shape and names, a *place* in his imagination for a fear he would have discovered, late if not soon.

People are the final fear, whether the "creatures" are from this world or another—the possibility, the threat of another's intervention or power to intervene in our lives, to hurt us and know they are hurting us, to choose to go on hurting us.

Evil. That is what Aaron fears. And he has discovered that evil is possible only where there are people. And because he cannot imagine any of the people he knows being evil, he has brought people from another place to populate his fear, given them green flesh, made them as different from himself as their motives are foreign to his comprehension.

Dr. Robert L. Dupont, director of the Phobia Program at the Institute for Behavior and Health in Washington,

D.C., says three factors govern fear: our ability to control a situation, the size of the event, and our familiarity with the threat.

According to Dupont's criteria, Aaron has every reason to be afraid. You can't control people from *this* world, much less from another. Likewise, beings and creatures from another world are an event of fearful proportions. Finally, Aaron is no more familiar with the creatures he imagines than he wants to be.

When he was four, I tried to teach Aaron the foolishness of a child's fear. And I thought the fear went away. But fear is a virus, active or dormant in us, but always there, waiting for a moment, an event, a shape through which to spring into activity. And Aaron may have discovered a fear that does not go away, a terror no phobia program can dispel, because the perception that breeds the fear is accurate.

The Scot philosopher John MacMurray contends that mature religion is not evidenced in believing God will prevent what we fear, but in knowing that what we fear may come, and still be *overcome,* still be endured. Sometimes children are brought safely through the sea on dry land, delivered from the Pharaoh they fear. But sometimes the sword is swifter than the grace that might have parried it; sometimes Herod comes, strong and terrible, like a being or creature from another planet.

The courage I taught Aaron when he was four—the courage of believing in protection and deliverance—is helpless against such knowledge.

So, I had Aaron get a sleeping bag from the basement,

and he slept the night of his nine-year-old fear through beside my bed.

But I did not sleep. I lay awake and watched the dark corners of the room, preparing myself for the beings and creatures I was certain would come.

The Evil

"Take your pillows and get inside," Aaron shouted. "The Evil is coming."

His sisters, Sarah and Patricia, excitedly obeyed, gathering up the cushions and blankets they had been using to play house. Then they all ran, screaming, toward the kitchen, where Marcia stood watching.

"Quick!" Aaron yelled as they all came through the kitchen door, heading for the stairs. "Hide under your beds; maybe The Evil won't find us there."

Evidently, it didn't, because an hour later Aaron was wandering back through the kitchen on his way outside.

Usually it is best to let Aaron just wander. It's one of the things he does best. You can tell him to do things, but wandering is what he'll end up doing, anyway. So, if you make up your mind that wandering is what you most want him to do, everyone is happy.

But Marcia was too curious not to ask him. "Aaron," she inquired, blocking his retreat to the yard, "what's The Evil?"

"Huh?"

"The Evil. You all ran inside to hide from it."

"Oh, we were just playing."

"Yes, I know. But what was it supposed to be."

"Nothing. It's just pretend."

"But what were you pretending it was?"

Aaron sighed. Aaron frequently sighs over our questions. It is as though he is bearing an enormous weight: the weight of our ignorance, our inability to understand things as they are. At least, as they are to him.

"It's just something to be afraid of," he insisted, "like when at church they say to be afraid of *the evil*. It's like that." And he was gone.

That evening Marcia told me about the incident. "He just said, 'It's like that,' and he was off to play. Isn't that strange?"

Yes. Strange.

But what is strange to all the world is perfectly reasonable to Aaron. He has the ability to reduce the most common event to bizarre detail, to see commonality in the most bizarre circumstance. It is his gift, the gift of his age. Nothing is impossible to him, and everything; whenever there is something "evil," there is some place to hide.

A few weeks after Aaron's confrontation with "The Evil," I had a confrontation of my own. A friend of ours died. She was young and healthy; there was no explanation for her death: she was a sports enthusiast who jogged daily, a beautiful woman with a young family. At the breakfast table buttering toast, she went pale and fainted. By the time the ambulance arrived, she was dead of a stroke.

Not only were we upset by her passing and concerned for her family, but the tragedy of the moment made us more cognizant of our own fragile existence. What would we do if such an unavoidable and terrible thing were to happen to one of us? How could I manage without Marcia? What would become of the children if we both were to die? Death is not the terror; the terror is the life death leaves behind: my life without Marcia; Marcia's life without me; the lives of our children without us. For family, the separation is the final grief, an abyss which even faith and love have difficulty spanning.

And yet, span it they must; span it they do. My father died when I was fourteen. In some ways, I still feel cheated. But I survived what I perceived to be "The Evil" of his passing to anticipate "The Evil" of my own.

More than what I *believe,* this has to do with what I *feel.* Aside from the hopes I have for what follows this life, I fear this life, fear what it can do to me and those I love.

"Take your pillows and get inside," Aaron had said. "The Evil is coming." He didn't mean death, or life. He wouldn't have been right if he had. But though life and death are not "The Evil," through them I know what Aaron means.

There are fears for which there are no beds to hide under. Even if we were to close our eyes and wait, there are things, events, "evils" that will be waiting for us when we look out again.

Dad Isn't the Groovy Type

We were driving home. Twilight. The fog glowed almost gold a few feet in front of the headlights. The children argued in the back seat about who had eaten the most three nights before. Twilight. The fog glowed . . . red from the tail lamps of a van turning left in front of us.

"You should get a car like that," Sarah said, too far down in the argument to prove having eaten as much, much less more. "You should get one like that, only orange; with red and yellow fire painted on it."

"No," Aaron (who could never eat as much as his older brother, Calvin) interrupted, "Dad's not the groovy type."

Indeed. But I was. I grew up dreaming of a candyapple-green street rod, jacked and raked, chromed exhaust pipes and hubcap spinners, white fur dice hanging from the rear-view mirror, suicide knob on the steering wheel, with a four-leaf clover laminated under plastic.

And it was to have yellow and red flames.

"Maybe I will," I told Aaron. "Maybe I will get a van for you kids to rattle around in, and paint it like Sarah says."

"Noooooooooo," Aaron laughed. "It would be too funny."

The fog misted green from the traffic signal, and the van disappeared in a swirl, fog closing gray behind its going.

Aaron leaned into the front seat and cocked his head to look at me. I kept my eyes on the road, but glanced at him. "You aren't really going to, are you?" he asked, smiling.

A few days before, we had talked about growing up. Calvin, who is thirteen, had been particularly anxious to know when the event is accomplished: at eighteen? nineteen? When does the responsibility to others end and the responsibility only to self begin?

I told him never. I told him that only the players change, not the activity.

Calvin was oblivious to the philosophy. "What I'm going to do is get my own apartment," he fantasized, "and a Ferrari. I'm going to get a red Ferrari."

A red Ferrari, perhaps with scalloped flames and chrome . . .

Aaron enjoyed the game and followed his brother's lead. "Me, too. I'm going to move out and get an apartment and a car."

Aaron requires not merely supervision but constant vigilance to sustain him even so long as from morning to evening without disaster. The idea of his moving into an apartment where he would care for himself requires more than a leap of imagination—it requires a reordering of the universe.

But it was only a game. So I asked him when he planned to make the move, and to where.

Aaron didn't want to think of practical applications; he wanted to dream of his brother's car. Nevertheless, he thought. And finally he said slowly, like someone reading a sign from a great distance, "I think I'll move out when I'm . . . twenty-seven. I'll buy that house that's for sale across the street from ours. That way, anytime you want to see me, you can just walk across the street."

Anytime we want to see him, or him us.

The fog settled heavy with the night, and our headlamps reflected off it as they would have off a wall.

Aaron strained even further into the front seat, wriggling against my shoulder as I strained to see. "Whataya say, Dad? Are you going to do what Sarah said? Are you going to get one of those?"

His face was dark in the dark car, but the slight illumination of the dash glowed almost gold on his cheeks and forehead.

"Maybe," I said, and he laughed, because I'm not the groovy type.

Although I can remember candyapple green, tuck-and-roll white Naugahyde upholstery, and the gold embrace of flames swept back and bright almost as a red Ferrari . . . or an orange van.

Sarah

A Child's Worth

Several days ago, Sarah tiptoed into my study and thrust her tightly clenched fist under my nose. "Wanna know what I've got in here?" she asked. Normally my study is off-bounds to the children, but it is difficult for Sarah to understand normal boundaries, or anything else normal. You may know a child like her—no matter how hard you try, the urchin always manages to amaze, confuse, and frustrate you. This time, however, I vowed that it would be different: I would not be surprised; in short, I would not allow her to win.

"Hey, ya wanna know what I've got in here?" she persisted, waving her white-knuckled little fist in my face.

"Sure," I said, in as composed a voice as a father whose territory has just been violated can muster. "Sure I do. Just what *do* you have in there?"

"I got two flies, a lizard tail, and three black and yellow things I don't know what they are. Ya wanna see?"

It was no use; she had won again. I knew it, and I suspect child psychologists would confirm my suspicion that somewhere in her heart of hearts, she knew it too.

But in the final analysis, my real problem doesn't lie so much in the fact that I am unable to stay ahead of Sarah, as that I feel a need to. I don't mean the normal and healthy need good parents feel to protect a child from inexperience. I mean that generally unconsidered need most of us occasionally feel to protect ourselves from our children.

I'm no psychologist; and I don't have the ability or desire to explain the phenomenon. But I suspect it has something to do with competition and the fact that parents all too often fail to recognize their children as peers—creatures for whom they are responsible but who, like themselves, are here either to fulfill or to fail in their lives.

Volumes have been filled with platitudes and homilies sappy people have invented to describe the gentle nature, elegant simplicity, and innocence of children. But the fact is that Sarah drives me crazy. She won't eat what is put on her plate but will happily consume whatever the dog leaves in his dish; she has a passion for bugs and other creatures that terrorize her mother and me; she has no sense of shame and is only too happy to take treats from whoever offers them, and she requests them from those who don't; she has managed to disrupt virtually every occasion she has attended—from church meetings to grade school carnivals —since the day she was born.

But the other things are true of her too. She is gentle, and that same youth which gives her recklessness and error also gives her innocence. The bugs she had to show me had been quite thoroughly crushed, but it was not out of any wretchedness or anger that their tiny existences had been ruined—rather, a complex of Sarah's innocence and gentle desire to possess them, perhaps even to love them, had produced the error.

But under normal circumstances I would have seen it only as an error—an error which infringed on my time and delicate sensibilities. Under normal circumstances, I would have punished her and hoped that she had learned her lesson.

And children *do* need to be disciplined; they *do* need to be protected against their own naiveté and a world which would destroy them. But how have my punishments been designed more to protect me than them?

Recently my eldest child, Calvin, was nearly run over by a tractor that was excavating at our neighbor's home. It was the sort of thing that might have been expected of Sarah—clowning for friends in an impossibly dangerous way—but Calvin was old enough to know better. It happened while I was away, but when I got home and was told of the experience by that neighbor, sick with terror and concern I stormed to the upstairs bedroom, where my son had been sent by his mother. Throwing open the door with all the anger that fear can produce, I found him, his knees pulled up tight against his chest and clasped between his arms. His head was down, and although I could hear no sound, as his body rocked back and forth I could see that he was quietly sobbing.

I was not prepared for it. It had not occurred to me that he would be as upset as I. Nor could I, standing in the doorway of his room, understand how or why he should be so moved. My anger was displaced by confusion, as it so often had been with Sarah, and, without touching him, I asked him what was wrong. "Daddy," he said, "I've done a stupid, stupid thing."

Suddenly the horror was no longer that I so nearly lost him, but that I had so nearly lost him without knowing how far he had come towards being what I wanted him to be. "Daddy," he cried, "I know that it wouldn't be so bad to die. I'd get to see Grandpa Jolley and be with God and find out the answers to all those questions you say we'll have to wait till we get to heaven to find out and all that stuff. The trouble is that most people die after they've grown up, and when all those old people in heaven saw me there they'd want to know why a little boy like me died, and I'd have to tell them it was because I did that stupid, stupid thing."

I didn't know how correct his doctrine was; I did know that he had won. But if the picture of him sitting in a corner, wound in his own grief, had not been so pathetic, I might have done what I usually do, and the knowledge of my son as a thinking, feeling, significant human being would have had to wait for another time, if it were to come at all.

Yet there was no reason it has to wait so long. If I had believed, in spite of formal failures, the essential doctrine stumbled on by the sentimentalists about the innocence and the importance and, yes, even the wisdom of children, I might have watched my son grow to accountability instead of suddenly realizing he was accountable. Or perhaps I did "believe" but had never believed deeply enough for it to have a positive place in my life. Whatever went wrong, some sense failed to move from where I think to where I am—a sense for my children and your children: the children that are ours; the children that we were, and, if we are wise, will be again.

So I didn't spank Sarah, and I nearly lost Calvin, and now I believe, occasionally. But perhaps it is too occasional, too infrequent. If my children are to become what I believe is possible for them, and if I really believe—not merely give Sunday-lip-service to an abstract philosophical principle, but really believe—then I must respond to that belief and more regularly regard my children with that respect and genuine concern which will ultimately displace the sense of trouble and burden they occasionally produce in me. If I am to love them truly, they must be more than merely charges: they must be companions as well.

Recently, I taught for a few months in England. Returning home, Marcia and I found ourselves on a busy platform of Victoria Station with all the children present and accounted for—except for Sarah. Sarah, who had for six months begged gum from waistcoated British gentlemen (who would not have been caught dead with a stick of the stuff on their persons); Sarah, who had never been able to ride on the subway without at least once breaking free from her father's careful grip and running up and down the silent rows singing "I Am a Child of God"; Sarah, who was at all times impossible to ignore *or* understand, was now quite suddenly gone. As I think about it now, it seems curious that I did not at least briefly think how much more quiet and simple the world would be with her gone; but of course I did not. All that I felt was how unessential other things would be without her. Then as I looked down the long flight of stairs we had just come up, I saw a very little, very old English lady struggling up the stairs, a struggle made no easier by the dwarf-like American child in her arms and clinging to her throat.

I rushed down the stairs and took Sarah from her. "Thank you very much," I said, "you really shouldn't have."

"Actually," she responded, "I didn't have much choice —the child insisted."

And so she continues to insist. She insists herself upon my mind, and, because there is a disparity between what she is and what the sentimentalists say she should be—because there is an occasional disparity between what I feel for her and the way I treat her—because of these and other frailties of herself and myself, she continues to insist her way upon my conscience.

Last night Sarah rushed into my study again—no bugs in her hands, but the sound of insects in her ears.

"Listen, Daddy; do you hear the crickets? Can you hear what they say? They say, 'Sarah-Sarah, Sarah-Sarah.' "

And so they do.

Beauty and the Blank Wall

The greatest creative failure of the coloring book industry is in not being able to design a book that Sarah finds so tempting, so alluring, so in need of crayon coloring as the walls of our home.

No matter how I threaten or encourage, the temptation of all that broad, tall, white, empty space is ultimately too much for Sarah's imagination. Although weeks may go by of total remission from her compulsive need to fill all the doors and sidings of our house with her "art," it is only a matter of time and opportunity before the beginnings of a new masterwork appear.

Her newest mural is located in the hall outside her room. I had recently made a serious point of instructing the children about the need to respect and care for our home. So, when Marcia told me that our "artist" had been at it again, I decided it was time for a father-daughter discussion about obedience and self-control.

"You know that we have a rule against writing on the walls, don't you?"

"Yes," she responded, paying more attention to a fly buzzing against the window than to me.

"Look at me when I speak to you," I scolded. And she did, briefly. "Is there a rule against it?"

She nodded.

"Then why did you break our family rule and write on the walls?"

She did not answer, and I launched into what I had been waiting to tell her about how difficult it is to wash crayon off walls and how hard her mother works to keep the house clean and how many little girls there are who would kill to live in a nice house like hers. (At very least, those little girls would be willing to promise never to write on the walls!)

Then I clinched it: I described a few of the terrifying punishments I was going to inflict on her if she disobeyed.

"Now," I concluded, "do you promise never to write on the walls ever again?"

"Yes," she covenanted. And that was that.

Until a little more than a week ago.

"Remember that scribble we haven't washed off the wall yet?" Marcia asked as I came in from mowing the lawn. "Well, your daughter has added to it."

I believe that somewhere in the Bible it says that you can stone disobedient children to death. I wouldn't want to do that. Just enough to bruise them well would be fine.

I went downstairs to my daughter's room, the patriarchal fires of presumably righteous indignation raging in my breast. And as I passed "the wall," I paused to let my anger cool as I assessed the most recent scribbling.

But it wasn't scribbling at all. It was a picture. What I had thought was no more than green and purple circles and thrusts was, quite suddenly, a picture—a picture of a face. True, it was a green and purple face—not what I would have chosen to go with the rust carpet—but it was a face, and my daughter had made it so by adding the mouth and eyes it had lacked since we caught and stopped her in the middle of its creation.

A number of years ago, when Marcia and I visited Rome, one of our most moving experiences was an excursion to the catacombs. There, beneath the Appian Way, we marveled at the stone walls where ancient Christians had etched their names and the symbol of their faith: a fish. Because their living and their dying was confined, they reached out to their confinement and wrote themselves upon it and painted their faith as a window to the world above.

Recently, I returned to the mountain camp where my father had taken me in the early 1950s; I found the fallen redwood where we had carved our names, and I ran my fingers across the uneven scarring of the massive trunk. I showed my children the memento of my father's and my own graffiti, and I told them about the man their grandfather had been; and I told them what it was like to stand with him beside a tree so much larger than ourselves and mark it for our own. And together, my children and I carved our names, renewing the ritual, preserving ourselves into a time when I hoped they would return with children of their own.

I am happy that no hand reached out to stop those early Christians, and that my father had us carve our names where they would not be lost or thrown away. And I am happy to have a daughter who shares my need for permanence and size, a daughter who cannot bear to live with a face (of whatever color) that lacks a mouth and eyes.

Such a need in one so young does complicate my life. Sarah is no Michelangelo, and I am not prepared to surrender all my walls (or any of my ceilings) to her.

But I have given her one. It's the one outside her bedroom door.

So far it has a green and purple face, a yellow house, and a lot of small, dark things I hope are horses or dogs. It doesn't move me in the way the Saint Sebastian Catacomb did, but it moves me. And every now and again, when she takes me down to show me what she has created in the dimly lit interiors of our home, I remember the catacombs, and the grand and rotting redwood of my childhood.

And one wall in a basement hallway seems almost too little room for growing up on.

Creativity vs. Lying

"I have bad news from Sarah's teacher," Marcia told me. And I thought, *Little wonder!*

Sarah is the sort of child about whom it is difficult to imagine a teacher calling with good news; unless in a fit of ecstasy a teacher were to telephone and chortle, "The most amazing thing happened today: Sarah was no trouble at all!"

I may have more encouraged than repaired Sarah's eccentric behavior. Since she was born, Sarah has been a wonder. Forever entertaining, always a surprise, she has become one of the indispensable joys of my life. I cannot remember what I did for amusement before she came along.

But what amuses me bothers teachers. The very things that make her run when I am energetic make her impossible when a teacher is tired; because while the world grinds grudgingly onward—sinking through entropy into constant change—Sarah is constant. Sarah is a world of life collapsed into a single vessel, a dark star made bright by inalterable will. All about her is mutable, while she is always what she was and *will be* what she is.

"Her teacher said she lied," Marcia said, whispering the last word.

"What?"

"She lied. Her teacher says that Sarah lied to her."

Sarah does not lie. Sarah invents; Sarah enlarges; Sarah embellishes the fact. Sarah does not lie.

Sarah has been blessed with a creative nature that anticipates possibilities. Is this not what Picasso did? And Rembrandt? And all true artists? Sarah is simply a poet. At very least she is a performer. What else is there to do when one's script is inadequate to one's talent? Occasionally, one must ad lib.

"She was just being creative," I corrected Marcia.

"She told her teacher that her mother was dead and her only sister had been burned alive. But her teacher had seen me, so Sarah told her that I was the stepsister who forced her to do all the work at home, which is why she hadn't finished her studies for school."

"Oh!"

"She claimed to have been born in Italy, to have been raised in France, and to be able to speak five foreign languages, when she is in the mood, which she hasn't been lately."

Have I mentioned how imaginative Sarah is? Well, she is. Very. Sarah is imaginative; and as is the case with all children, her imagination reveals her need.

"We mustn't become hysterical about these clever inventions," I told Marcia. "We must ask ourselves, What do we learn from these tales? What is Sarah trying to tell us? What made her feel so hostile towards *you* and her brothers and sisters?"

"Me? What do you mean by that?"

"Well, she must have had some reason for doing away with you and the others. Children do not say such things unless they have some reason, unless there is some substance on which to base the character and nature of their mythology. It all means something, doesn't it?"

This, I was sure, was excellent psychology. I was beginning to feel very broad-minded and mature.

"Then what do you suppose she meant," Marcia asked, "when she told her teacher that you ran away with a fan dancer and died while performing as a tattooed man in a carnival sideshow?"

I felt hysteria rising in me like a blush. And for the first time I realized where *invention* leaves off and *lying* begins: just this side of Sarah's inventions about me!

Pretty Girls

Sarah's picture was of three little girls. You could tell they were girls, because their hair was curly and their stick legs protruded from triangle skirts.

She had worked hard on the picture; it had many colors. Two of the little girls were smiling; the third was crying, the corners of her mouth pointing at the bottom corners of the page.

The first photograph I ever saw of Marcia as a child was a black-and-white snapshot taken of her at the beach. She was about four years old, a few years younger than Sarah. Her hair hung in blonde, Shirley Temple curls, and she smiled largely into the silent camera.

"What an interesting picture," Marcia said when Sarah showed her the trio she had worked so hard on.

Marcia learned somewhere that one does not ask a child *what* a picture *is*. One says, "My, what beautiful colors," or, "Look at all those lovely lines." One comments on the accomplishment rather than demanding definitions. One does not wish to threaten a creative instinct with perceptual challenges or demands for realism.

"What an interesting picture," Marcia said. "What is it?"

"What?" Sarah responded.

"Well, not *what*, actually. I can see *what* it is: It's a picture of three little girls, isn't it? What I really wanted to know is *why?* Why are these two little girls smiling and the other one frowning?"

In the snapshot, three decades grayer than when it was taken, Marcia sits in the sand, poorly framed by an inexperienced photographer.

Her right leg extends to the picture's right border, where her right foot is severed by the edge of the print. Her left leg is tucked under her, the knee reaching the bottom border, where half the kneecap is clipped.

Between her legs is a tin bucket and shovel, the painted anchor on the pail half rusted away.

"You see," Sarah explained, "this one is sad and crying because she is ugly. The other two are happy because they are pretty. And they aren't girls, they're flowers."

Marcia tells me that she grew up thinking that she was pretty. Everyone told her so. Aunts, uncles, older cousins —they all said she was "cute," "the sweetest little thing."

But what the photograph shows is an ordinary little girl with a chipmunk face whose mother fussed over her too much. A chipmunk of a little girl who has been told that she was pretty.

"The sun is frowning, too," Marcia continued. "Why is the sun unhappy?"

"Because he's alone. The two happy flowers are pretty, so they have each other. But the sun is all alone."

There should be a rule. An unbreakable rule. Little girls should all think they are pretty—until they are seventy-five. At least until they are nine.

Mothers should fuss over them. Aunts and uncles should congratulate them. Everyone should love them. Or leave them alone.

Of course, there *are* more important things than being pretty. There are always more important things. But maybe not for a little girl whose suns do not smile, who can see the flowers that do not have friends for not being pretty.

Maybe for a little girl, being pretty is a symbol, an emblem of those other, more important things. The philosopher Immanuel Kant said as much. He believed "the Beautiful" to be the symbol of "the Good."

In Marcia's case, he was right. From the incompletions of a scarred and poorly posed photograph, she has grown into a woman of remarkable emotional completion.

And when I tease her about the snapshot, about the little girl that she was, she says: "It doesn't matter. Not anymore.

What is important is that when I was little, I *believed* what I was told; and because of what I was told, I believed that I was loved, that I was worthwhile.''

All that from being pretty, in the minds and mouths of others.

You can't love a child *too* much, you don't spoil her by telling her she's pretty. You can only restore what the world tries to amputate; you re-frame the photograph and make her whole.

Sarah, you are beautiful. More beautiful than you can know. Certainly no less pretty than flowers and sun, or a little girl playing with a rusty pail in the sand.

With Turtles and with Children, It Is Not Easy to Know

"The flowers appear on the earth; the time of the singing of birds is come, and the voice of the turtle is heard in our land."

—Solomon's Song 2:12

With a turtle, it is not easy to know.

Not entirely because of the shell. But the shell does not make it easier. Nor does the turtle's beaked and toothless mouth that remains the same, its flesh already green, its disinclination to move.

It is not easy to know when a turtle is dead.

A dead turtle does not float belly up in a fish bowl, does not drop to the bottom of a cage; turtles do not collapse when they die, because they are so very nearly collapsed when they are alive.

So, we are not certain how long Sarah's turtle had been dead. It had not moved for a very long time. But it frequently did not move, then moved. This is what distinguishes a turtle from a Chihuahua. This, and the shell.

So much about a turtle is so much the same when he is dead as when he is alive, that it is possible for even a turtle that is close to you to die and for you not to notice for a long time.

Even a turtle you named Tommy.

Tommy Turtle is survived by Sarah (who owned him) and by an unnamed goldfish (who is also owned by Sarah, and whose days are probably numbered).

So that you will not think us inattentive who do not know the day and hour (or even the week) of his death, I will tell you that Tommy's stomach shell was very red, the shell across his back an agate green; and the flesh along his throat was soft where Sarah touched it to teach Tommy the only trick he knew: opening his mouth.

When Tommy did not move for so very long, Sarah thought it was a second trick.

In a way it was.

We would have buried Tommy beneath the cherry tree where we buried the kitten run over by a car. But this winter the ground was frozen and the snow drifted deep against the fence in the backyard. And Tommy was not a turtle to stand on formalities.

We wrapped him in a plastic garbage sack and set him out to be picked up with the trash.

Sarah tried to take it bravely. But again and again the moment returned to her: our knowing Tommy was dead. "I didn't know turtles died," she said. "Not like the guppies we flushed down the toilet. I thought turtles lived as long as us."

And so they do. Some longer. Some just as long. Some just as short.

Their dying is less an inconvenience than our own—partly because it is so difficult to know, partly because it seems to make so little difference to the turtle—but otherwise, turtles die like us; and you can't be certain to keep a turtle any more than you can keep a child.

I cannot write this without thinking there is a moral in it. But moralizing seems inappropriate with Tommy wrapped in a trash sack and not yet picked up with the trash. But moralizing is no more inappropriate than our makeshift burial of so good and silent a friend, who was so content with lettuce leaves, and who never failed to open his mouth when Sarah pushed against his throat. Moralizing is certainly no less appropriate than the sack in which we shrouded Tommy. But there was no avoiding the sack, and turtles understand necessity.

But as good a turtle as Tommy was, he might not understand our turning moral profits from his final trick, our finding meaning more meaningful than the red across his undershell that faded to orange even as we gingerly lifted him a final time.

With a turtle, it is not easy to know the moment of death; even when the turtle's name is Tommy. But once you know, a name is not so important as the moment.

And the moment is more important than any moral we might make of it.

Rachel

Miss Professor
Explains the World

I was sitting in the bathtub.

There are many things for which age creates a need. A bathtub is one of them. You can run around in a shower when you're young; but by the time middle age looms its hoary head, you need some way to get clean that doesn't require exercise.

And someplace just to sit and be warm.

I was sitting in the bathtub, being warm, when Rachel marched in. (The single disadvantage of a bathtub is that it is more conducive of audiences than are showers. People who would never think of talking to you over the cascading roar of a shower are ever-so-pleased-and-thank-you-very-much to sit down next to the bathtub and tell you their troubles.)

Rachel was wearing one of her mother's suits. Dragging

it, actually. Her arms, legs and neck all poked through in the right places, more or less; but most of the yardage dragged behind her. And as she wade-marched into the bathroom, her sister Sarah declared from the other room: "Here comes Miss Professor!"

Professor, indeed! Since I was once a teacher myself, I am jealous of the dignity attending the office of "professor." I knew that a clumsy aping of academic sartorialia and a false claim to academic insight could only get Rachel in trouble.

What was clear (besides the invasion of my bath) was that Miss Professor needed a swift lesson on the responsibilities of her pretense.

"You're a professor?" I asked, rhetorically. "So, say something intelligent."

Rachel reached across her body and grasped her right elbow with her left hand, and with her right hand she stroked her chin. "Let me think," she pondered.

"Think?! Professors shouldn't have to think. Professors should have wisdom on the tips of their tongues, ready to spill out proverbs like peas from a tin. So, go ahead, Miss Professor. Just blurt out the first thing that comes to mind," I told her, covering my face with a washrag.

"Even the gods are helpless in the face of ignorance."

I swallowed the rag.

"What was that!"

"I said, even the gods are helpless in the face of ignorance."

My word! She *was* Miss Professor!

"I read it in one of your books," she smugly replied. "And Mr. Johns at school says it all the time."

I tried to imagine Mr. Johns. I wondered whether he took showers or baths. Baths, I was certain. I could imagine Mr. Johns sitting in a bathtub, confronted by the twenty or thirty Rachels in his class, and saying, "Even the gods . . ."

"He says that, and other things. Like, 'Cleanliness is next to godliness.' He says that, too."

Not as interesting a thing to say as the other. More common. Although, said from a bathtub, it might take on authority.

"Very interesting," I told Rachel, sincerely. "Do you know what it means?"

"About being clean?"

"No, the other."

"Oh, that. Sure. Miss Professor knows everything."

"So what does it mean?"

"Miss Professor knows; but Miss Professor doesn't always tell. If you give it all away, then you're out of a job."

She knew more about teaching than I had guessed.

"But for you, I'll make an exception. It means that when you know a lot, it's hard to explain what you know to somebody who doesn't know much. Right?"

Right. More or less.

The water in the bathtub was cold, and I with it. I debated letting a little of the cold water out and some warm in, or just getting out.

"You want Miss Professor to tell you anything else before I take off Mom's clothes?"

I looked at Rachel, swaddled in her mother's suit and wiser than I had thought her to be. *This is how it begins,* I thought, *and this is how it ends.* "Yeah. Should I get out of the bathtub or stay in?"

"Stay in," she replied without needing to think. "Cleanliness is next to godliness."

Ballet, Tap, and Baseball

"A ballerina lifts her leg above her head, bends backward over herself and stands on the tips of her toes—all abilities not allocated to the male physique. Our feet are more flexible than men's and are therefore able to arch enough to be 'over' our pointes. It raises our height four or five inches so that we see eye to eye with our male counterparts. And yet, while we are equalized in this way, we are there by way of strength and will, and our cause is beauty."
> —Toni Bentley, ballerina with the New York City Ballet, in *Rolling Stone*, 29 September 1983

My sister Valerie studied tap dance. I remember her dancing in the bandstand of a park somewhere in the California Verdugo hills. She carried a black cane, wore a black derby and black mesh stockings. Her cheeks and lips were rouged. She was eight years old.

Since before Rachel started school, she has studied ballet. For a time I had been worried; she acquired a pair of oversized tap shoes from a garage sale somewhere and went clunking around the house, chewing up the floors; I was afraid she would want to take tap lessons. Not that there is anything wrong with tap dancing; but I remembered Valerie, and that she was not very good at it, and that I was a little embarrassed by the black stockings. And I imagined Rachel dancing in black stockings in the foyer of some mall with twenty or thirty other eight-year-olds, and I was relieved when one evening, after seeing Swan Lake on PBS, she asked to take ballet. Ballerinas so seldom wear derbies.

Someone should have warned me.

My experience has been that when a child takes ballet, parents are in for a serious experience. This is not piano lessons once a week and force-her-to-practice-in-between; ballet is a vocation, a call, a holy enterprise; ballet is devotion to the formal accomplishment, a quest for the beauty a body can shape in air.

Ballet is to become an eight-year-old nun.

"We, as dancers, are in service. . . . We are embarked on the quest to lose ourselves to a higher perfection."
—Toni Bentley

"Daddy, we've got to go now."

"No, we have a few minutes before your lesson starts."

"No, we don't. Micki insists we be on time."

I also insist; on many things. But I do not get most of the things for which I insist. Perhaps because I do not carry a staff with which to thump the hardwood floor beneath the *barre;* perhaps because I cannot go *en pointe,* as can Micki.

"Madame Felia Doubrovska was perfect. . . . She would waft into the classroom the appropriate ten minutes late. . . . She was tall and delicate and elegant. She never walked. She ran and skipped on her demitoes, from the doorway across the studio to the piano, where she would quickly swirl around and land half-posed, one foot pointed."—Toni Bentley

When Sarah turned eight years old, she made a choice: not between tap and ballet, but between ballet and slow-pitch softball. She chose softball ("because that's more unusual; every girl I know is taking ballet") , and again I was relieved. Sure, you can be devoted to softball: you can buy a glove, stuff a wad of gum in your cheek, and pull your cap low over your eyes the way you see it done on TV. But you don't go around talking about the "higher perfection" of a three-run homer or the "spiritual nature" of slow pitch.

Sarah was pretty good at softball. She got a few hits, ran a few bases, and learned a few new words to call the teams her team lost to. But this year she gave up her brief career as a ballplayer, invested several weeks' allowance to buy pink slippers, and is taking ballet.

I don't think she'll be so devout as Rachel; it isn't in

Sarah's nature. But already she is beginning to call the shapes of her body by French names, learning the catechism of her order. Already she is beginning to point her toes as she walks; already she is talking about shoes that will make her as tall as I am.

Rachel was a cookie in this season's performance of the *Nutcracker*. She was a beautiful cookie, and I was proud of her. But cookies do not go *en pointe*. Cookies have mice nibble at their arms.

And I am spending more time than usual in shopping malls, watching little girls in derbies thump out the rhythm to "Toot-toot-tootsie, Good-bye," and wondering . . .

Rachel Defends Reincarnation

"Do you believe in reincarnation?" she asked without looking up from the dishes she was rinsing.

Rachel is twelve. She clears the table after evening meals. She loads the dishwasher. And she wonders.

The wondering used to be simpler. "I wonder why . . ." she would begin, and you knew the question would have something to do with why she should be the one to clear the table, or why she should have to go to bed before her older brother.

But now that she is nearly twelve, her wondering has turned metaphysical.

"What do you think? Is it possible?"

"I think not," I replied.

"How come?"

"Well, because the idea of reincarnation doesn't square with my religious philosophy."

"You mean you don't believe in reincarnation because somebody told you not to?"

I liked it better when Rachel wondered about bedtimes.

"No. No one told me not to believe the way I don't believe; I just *do* believe the way I do."

I had the uneasy feeling that Rachel's questions were beginning to make more sense than my answers.

"Well, I think maybe I do believe in reincarnation. It just makes sense. It's like riding on a merry-go-round, you know? Some people only get one ride; some people get two. Like that. So, that way the people who didn't get a good ride the first time, they get a second chance."

I think a merry-go-round defense of a metaphysical proposition is unique. I was nearly as pleased with Rachel's logic as I was troubled by her theology.

"Yes," I responded, "that makes a lot of sense. If having things make sense were enough to make them true, then the sense you've made of reincarnation would make it true."

"Things have to not make sense to be true?" Rachel asked.

"Of course not. I mean, a lot of things that are true make perfect sense; but some things that make sense are not true. It's like in a debate: a good argument may win the debate, but winning doesn't make the argument true."

What I was saying was proving itself to be true by making as little sense as possible. Certainly, I wasn't winning any arguments.

"Besides," I lamely continued, "you're assuming that

coming back to this life is a good thing. The Eastern religions that accept reincarnation believe that the best thing is to escape the wheel of karma, to not be reborn into a world that is so full of pain."

"Is that why you don't believe in it? You think life is terrible?"

"No! Of course not. I like my life very much."

"Exactly. And I think it would be a nice thing to be able to come back to it. Especially if you were born a long time ago and could come back now. I think those are mainly the people who are going to be reincarnated—the ones who haven't had the chance to see all the things we've seen and do the things we've done."

Remarkable. Rachel has structured an entire theology based upon the single proposition that everyone should be allowed to go to Disneyland, no one should miss seeing *Star Wars.*

"Perhaps the quality of life cannot be judged solely on the basis of conveniences and amusements," I told her. "Perhaps the people who lived a thousand years ago had every bit as much opportunity to live and love and make worthwhile contributions."

"You mean you wouldn't mind living back when they didn't have hot running water or indoor toilets or penicillin?"

"Well, no . . . I'm very happy to be living right now . . ."

"That's right. And if you didn't live right now it would only be fair to give you a chance to, which maybe somebody did, which is why I believe in reincarnation."

Rachel had finished clearing the table, triumphantly.

And I consoled myself with the hope that this was not an argument I needed to win. She was right for feeling the fairness of new beginnings, for believing in opportunity come round again.

I picked up the dish rag and went over a few spots she had missed, a few smudges on the shiny top of the table that I rubbed until the surface was perfectly clean.

A Plan to Save Russia

"I'm going to save Russia," Rachel said.

One might quibble. One might suggest there are logistics to be considered: the practical issue of distance, the expense of transportation, the difficulty of communication, not to mention the complication of resistance—Russia may not wish to be saved.

But in the face of a twelve-year-old's determination, these are no more than quibbles.

Rachel went *en pointe,* her leg warmers pushing wool against the blue bunching of Levi's at her knees, and as she arched her arms, she turned her head slightly to the left, looking to a far corner of the room in a classical pose, and she said again, "I'm going to save Russia."

She had been researching a report for school, learning about the Baltic and Georgian states, the early suppression by the Cossacks, the later suppression of the

Cossacks; the early suppression by the Czars, the later suppression by the Soviets—a panorama of autocracy and suffering so vast that she was at once overwhelmed and inspired.

What is one to respond to such ambition? What is one to say that will not sound petty or unimaginative? One does not wish one's children to be defeated by setting goals too high to be accomplished. On the other hand, saving Russia is not a bad idea.

"That's nice," I lamely answered.

"You don't think I can do it," Rachel shot back, thumping down on her heels, all the classicism collapsing from her tone and manner, denim taking over. "You don't think I can do it, do you?"

"Well, Russia is a very big place. . . ."

"That's what they told Gandhi!"

What in the world does Gandhi have to do with Russia?

"That's what they told Gandhi when he went to make salt!"

Let us turn aside a moment from Gandhi, Russia and salt. Let us suppose that the universe is a mature, well-ordered, sensible place in which it is possible to proceed from one point of discussion into the next without becoming confused. Let us suppose that the logic by which we purchase toothpaste is the same intellectual process by which we might figure a way to save Russia.

Toothpaste, salt and Gandhi aside, let us suppose . . .

"They told Gandhi there was no way. They told him India would never be free. So, he just up and marched to the sea, and all of India marched with him."

In 1930 Gandhi protested the British tax on salt by walking two hundred miles to the ocean, where he made his own salt, for which he was imprisoned.

"Of course they put him in jail! But what difference did that make? They had to let him out, didn't they? They had to! Because he was a great man. That's how I'm going to do it. That's how I'm going to save Russia. I'll get there, and the people will know why I've come, and together we'll march to the sea."

Let us turn aside a moment from logic. Let us assess the progress logic has made, and for a moment let us suppose that a twelve-year-old ballerina could do no worse. The Baltic is no less salty than the Indian Ocean, the Kremlin prisons no more sternly walled than the British jails unable to keep Gandhi. Let us suppose that the universe is not so logical as ideal, that the gravitational center the planets spin around is a man, or a twelve-year-old girl in leg warmers. . . .

"No one believes me. But that doesn't matter. They didn't believe Gandhi, and he made salt, just the same."

Just the same.

Let us be reasonable. Let us be logical. Let us agree: Russia is in for a hard time.

A Chain of
Love and Suffering

When I was six, polio hit me. I spent four months in the hospital and two years without walking, and ended up with a pair of weak ankles and legs that still don't match. It was the most significant and enduring experience of my childhood. Polio taught me suffering—a lesson I had hoped to teach my children, vicariously.

Then yesterday, while I reported the first Hawaiian volcanic eruption in nearly two years, my son Calvin took a nose dive out of a coconut palm. He had seen the Polynesian children shinnying up and down the striated trunks, and he had gotten pretty good at copying them. But posing while his cousin took a picture, he had lost his grip and fallen nearly twenty feet, reaching out as he struck the ground and taking most of the impact on his hands and wrists.

By the time I got to him, Calvin was conscious but disoriented; he thought he was in Utah, and I wished he was. I wished he had been climbing scrub oak. (The scrub is a modest tree. It grows close to the ground, spreading, and has branches for climbing in and clinging to. You can fall out of scrub oak, but not without difficulty, and not far.)

Palm trees grow towards the sun in a single-minded devotion to their own purpose, providing neither shade nor access. And they punish those who seek to trespass on their solitude of height; punish them with a spare, unyielding stem that grows more difficult and dangerous as it ascends.

Calvin had climbed to the top, ascending like a blonde koala—his arms looping the trunk, his legs pumping him upwards in a rhythmic conquest. He had posed triumphant among the clusters of green coconuts, waving to his cousin, and had been swept out of the tree by a gusting of the Hawaiian trades. He fell twenty feet, without a single branch to break his fall.

The orthopedic surgeon who attended Calvin said it was fortunate he had reached out when he hit the ground. It is not uncommon in such a fall for the head to strike first, or the back. In such cases paralysis or death are the usual result. As it was, Calvin had broken both wrists at the growth plates; but although they were serious fractures, difficult to set, the doctor said they likely will mend without serious deformity.

Without *serious* deformity. I don't want Calvin to be deformed at all. I don't want him to feel any pain. He came to his mother and me without defect, unblemished; and I had planned to keep him that way.

But I haven't. His teeth slightly buck, he's scarred from numerous childish misadventures, his toes tuck in when he walks, and both his wrists are broken. Things which I might have prevented and things over which I have no control have combined to harm and change the body of my son from the perfect thing it was to what it is.

And what it is, is more dear to me. I know the history of each deformity, the reason for each blemish of his hide. I have taken him to the podiatrist, and the good doctor has assured us both that there are worse things than being pigeon-toed. Calvin will wear orthodontic braces until he's fifteen, because he has his mother's mouth; and as his mother did, he will bear with whatever grief braces bring.

What he is and will yet become is mine; he is part of me. His sufferings witness that fact. When he cut his leg on a broken bottle and collected four stitches for his pain, my legs ached all day. When he chipped his protruding front tooth—a permanent one—I began again to tongue the lower cuspid I had chipped years before. And last night, his wrists broken and suspended in casts above his head to keep his hands from swelling, I sat beside him as he tossed and tried to sleep, and I did not sleep. What I suffered when a child has taught me the terror in suffering. Just so, his suffering shall teach him.

Nevertheless, it is an even more difficult lesson to watch than to learn. I would do anything to alleviate the pain Calvin is feeling—even take it on myself.

The suffering I most dread belongs to me only through those I love.

George Orwell indicates the failure of this phenomenon in his apocalyptic novel *1984,* when Winston cries out in his fear of rats, "Do it to Julia." This failure to love, to be willing to suffer for love, is the antithesis of what suffering is designed to teach us—that there is nothing so terrible but that love may overcome it. This lesson learned, we are united as families, parents and children, in a chain of love and suffering that reaches forward to our children, and backwards to one who loved and suffered for us all.

Last night, as Marcia smoothed Calvin's hair, she told him, "Dad has bad ankles, and now you have bad wrists. You make quite a pair."

I hope she's right.

A Simpler Solution
to the Puzzle of Rubik's Cube

Calvin was excited. "Look!" he virtually chortled, thrusting the plastic, varicolored cube into my face. "It's a Rubik, the real thing!"

I had hoped that a year of Space Invaders, of watching electronic blips floating on a black nimbus, had saturated the neurosynaptic links of his brain; I had hoped that our family might be spared *The Cube*.

I had known about the Rubik for quite some time, had been quietly cutting all mention of it out of the newspapers and magazines delivered to our home, had quickly changed the channel when any mention of it was made on television.

I figured that the world is a complicated enough place without increasing the frustration by allowing a puzzle that has 43,252,003,274,489,586,000 positions ("but only one solution," according to the Ideal Toy Corp.)

into our home. I figured I should protect my children from a game designed to teach them how futile are their efforts, how feeble their imaginations.

I am quite certain that frustrations such as Rubik's Cube are designed to destroy the American family. I know, it seems a preposterous proposition. But when Douglas R. Hofstadter hailed the Cube in *Scientific American* as the new plaything of the intelligentsia, he advised his readers to plan on spending between five hours and a year in trying to solve the puzzle.

Well, what's going to happen to those people's families while they are working out the solution? And what will happen if they don't discover the solution? Statistics have not yet been compiled on how many promising young scientists have been driven mad by frustrations such as the Cube provides, but the figures must be staggering!

So, while undermining the foundations of American family life, Rubik's Cube is also making a firm assault on the vitality of the American scientific community. Even if most of our scientists are not driven mad by it, an enormous amount of their time is consumed. While they could be curing cancer, our scientists are trying to position the last of the nine yellow squares.

But I am not a scientist. My primary concern is for the family, for *my* family. Rubik's Cube inevitably destroys the respect children have for their parents and for adults in general. While Hofstadter is advising Ph.D. physicists to take a year out for the Cube, Jonathan Cheyer became a Champion Cubist for solving the puzzle in 48.31

seconds. He is nine years old. The runners-up were Jeffrey Varasano (fourteen years old, 51.16 seconds) and Herbert H. Thorp (seventeen years old, 1 minute 09.64 seconds).

You see? The older you get, the slower you are. Adults have always known that to be true; but we've tried to keep it from the kids. Children need to believe that parents *know,* that they can *do.* But experts say that children are better at the Cube because their creative faculties are less inhibited.

"Here," Calvin challenged, "give it a try."

"Actually, my forte is in messing it up," I replied, spinning the cubes of the Cube in as many directions at once as I could. "Now, *you* try it."

That's the ticket. Turn the tables on them. Put *them* on the defensive. I smiled, patted my son on the head, and went to my study to write.

In three minutes he was standing at my desk, a perfectly ordered Rubik in his hand.

"Beginner's luck," I smiled a little nervously, spinning the sides another time. "Now go away, and don't come back until you get lucky again."

In two minutes he was back. Fantastic! All this time I had been worrying about Space Invaders rotting his brain, and I had this genius kid who had solved the Cube!

"Son," I said, drawing him to my bosom, "the world is going crazy trying to work this puzzle; what's more important, people are buying books to tell them how to solve it; people are paying *good money* for thin little books on how to do what you have done. Tell Daddy the secret so Daddy can make us rich."

"Simple," Calvin replied smilingly. "Instead of just spinning all the little cubes around and trying to make them work . . . ."

"Yes, yes?"

"If you pull really hard on the sides, the whole cube pops apart and you can just put it back together right. Simple, huh?"

The world each day slips deeper into the dark abyss of madness, its skids being greased by the Cube. And in all the ludicrous insanity of adults trying to retrieve the absolute clarity of youth, there is one glimmer of hope: no matter what Ideal says, there are *two* solutions. Rubik's and Calvin's.

Reinforcement

Calvin has broken his wrist. Again.

When he broke both wrists a little over a year ago, he was brave about it, but the arms had to be immobilized—both casts went over his elbows. He could pick things up, but since the casts would not allow his elbows to bend, he was unable to dress or feed himself, unable to bathe; unable to perform any of those simple, ambidextrous functions we take for granted.

Such immobility is at best an inconvenience. But for a boy who thinks the world revolves around "being coordinated," it was humiliating.

A few days after he returned to school with his two, bright white casts, everyone in his class received ice cream treats at the end of the school day. Calvin could not eat his, but he was too embarrassed to ask anyone for help. Instead, he bundled his books in one hand, the ice cream in the other, and ran for home. Home, where he knew there were people to help him.

It was a hot day. When Marcia opened the door, Calvin stood on the front step, the books at his feet, the soggy ice cream wrapper melted into the plaster of the cast, the ice cream gone.

Now, he had broken his left wrist again. "Just a coincidence," the doctor said. "This seems to have nothing to do with the last break."

He had been at an amusement park, in the Fun House, going around in a barrel, tumbling and turning with his friends like so many pebbles in a polishing drum.

So many pebbles . . . and one large stone: a fat woman who, as the barrel stopped, stepped on Calvin's wrist, and simply walked away.

"I don't think she knew," Calvin told me later. "But I sure did. I heard it crack, and when I looked down, I knew."

The wrist had been fractured through the growth plate. Again. Fractured, splinted, casted over the elbow: all as before.

"Well, at least I can feed myself," Calvin said, trying to cheer himself up. "And it isn't my right arm, so I can still write."

But his early attempts to be positive about his predicament quickly dissipated as the anesthetic wore off and the pain began to mount.

"Don't you remember," Marcia reassured him, "that

you finally decided you learned a lot when your arms were broken last time?"

"Like what?" he asked rhetorically, unwilling to be philosophical about his pain.

"Well, you said you learned a lot about suffering, so you would be able to be more sympathetic to the suffering of others."

"Yeah, but I learned that last time. So why do I have to go through it again? It's almost as though He did this to me on purpose."

Calvin knows better than that. Yet, there it was: what all of us, in spite of what we know, feel. The accident seemed too cruel a coincidence not to have purpose; it seemed planned; it seemed like He—God—had done it.

Calvin isn't like that. He's a good, religious boy. But maybe you can suffer just so much before your religious nature begins to wonder about suffering and its source. Even Job had to face down that question.

And even Job did not come up with an adequate answer.

"I don't know," Marcia told him. "Things just happen. Sometimes they just happen, and they're lousy, and there's nothing we can do about it. But that's no reason to blame God. God doesn't hurt people. It's fat ladies in barrels that do that. God is the one who makes it better, and bearable until it is."

Calvin picked at a piece of crumbling plaster with his right hand, rolled the gritty debris between his fingers, and said, "Yeah. I guess."

When I tell friends that Calvin has broken his arm again, they ask, "The same one?"

"Yes," I tell them, "the same."

But only one. There is that to be thankful for.

I know what Calvin is feeling. I feel it with him. There is no answer, no finally satisfying system by which the arbitrary grief of life may be resolved.

As we left the emergency room, the plaster still damp and warm on his arm, I asked: "Is there anything I can do?"

"Yeah," he said, "let's go get something to eat. And while we eat, let's not talk about how much I'm going to learn from this. OK?"

OK.

Children in a Gym

"He hit me, a bunch of times. In the stomach, the head. I told him to cut it out, but he just laughed. And his friends laughed."

Calvin wasn't so much upset as amazed. He told me what had happened, giving each detail a close attention inspired by sadness and shame.

We had gone for an evening swim at the gym. Calvin had practiced his diving, going many times into the pool, working on his approach to the board, his entry into the water. He is fiercely proud of his athletic skills, humiliated by his occasional failings. He is just beginning to anticipate those accomplishments which will allow him to believe that he is a man, those rites of passage that will teach him what it means to *be* a man.

And part of what he supposes it to mean is being "tough." And there are ways in which he is right.

"I told him to quit it, and he just hit me again. So I hit him back, but it was a mistake."

Calvin looked away, still not upset. If he were older, I would have thought he was being philosophical—philosophically melancholy. But Calvin was just sad, and ashamed.

"I don't even know why he did it. He just came up and said, 'Get out of the way,' and pushed me. And I told him not to, and he pushed me again. And again."

Calvin does not easily understand bad temper. He doesn't understand it in me, so he cannot understand it in a stranger; certainly not in a stranger his own size.

I tried to explain to Calvin that he had to learn to deal with this sort of thing, that there would always be people who would want to fight when he wanted to argue, want to argue when he wanted to discuss; that the world is full of near-savages who have only the slightest patina of civilization buffering them against the jungle of their own lives.

"But he took my things. When I went to tell the supervisor, this kid picked up my things and ran around the corner into the boys' locker room. I had everything rolled up in my towel—my card, my swimsuit, everything."

When you have been robbed, when you have been bullied, when the fragile rigging and freight of your manhood has been threatened, only action will do.

I looked at Calvin, and I knew what he wanted. Alone, he had failed. Alone, he had to go for help. What he wanted was for me to *help* him be what he thought a man should be, do what he thought a man should do. He wanted me to help him get *revenge.*

There is no explaining that will suffice against such need. All our holy books speak against such primitivism, to no avail. We *will* be avenged.

So I took Calvin by the hand, and we went after his attacker.

We found the boy in the locker room, where Calvin had seen him go. I was surprised to find how small he was, smaller even than Calvin, which is part of why Calvin was ashamed. The boy was small, but when he looked up at me, there was an anger in his eyes that made him large, an anger that had amazed and defeated Calvin.

We got back the card and the towel, and I made the boys shake hands. They didn't want to.

And as we drove home, I tried to explain as much of what had happened as I was myself able to understand; I tried to answer Calvin's question of "Why?"

Calvin nodded, but I don't think he understood. The world and his youth stand against his understanding. He can't help seeing such things—everywhere he looks, people are acting "tough" to protect the soft underbelly of their lives—but neither can he be expected to understand what it means. Even when he is grown, there will be people who continue to be frightened children in a gym, waging war, but with no adult intervention.

Perhaps he cannot understand that now. But he shall.

The Last Leaf

"I would order my cause before him, and fill my mouth with arguments."

—Job 23:4

Autumn is the time when the argument begins: the debate of whether the leaves will be raked, and when.

Calvin is responsible for raking the leaves, but in our old yard raking is a task that lasts all fall. First the weeping birch goes red, and then the maple turns yellow. Finally the bing cherry and apricot begin to drop their green as the grape leaves and vines turn brown, then gray.

"Before I can rake all the way across the yard, the places I've already raked are covered with leaves," Calvin complains. "It's no use! We should let all the leaves fall, then rake them all at once."

A sensible economy; make one job of it. But I explain

to Calvin the problem: a full fall of our leaves would make the sidewalk nearly impassable.

"I can rake the leaves from the walk back onto the lawn."

Fine. But there is no way to keep lawn leaves off the walk. The same winds that make raking so frustrating turn "lawn leaves" to "walk leaves," indiscriminately.

There is no alternative to raking, and bagging, and raking again.

But Calvin must be encouraged, constantly; and constantly he puts off the raking, then rakes a few half-hearted piles, becomes distracted, and returns to find the leafmeal scattered to where he had piled it from.

Calvin takes it as a sign: If God wanted leaves in piles, He'd make them fall that way.

One can argue against all causes but the providential. So, last autumn, halfway through the fall, I gave up encouraging and let Calvin work his own method of leaf gathering. The leaves piled and floated around our yard like golden waves of a parchment sea . . . around, and in. The children tracked crushed and crumbling elm leaves through the house; the dog came in with birch leaves clinging to his coat, which he immediately shook, scattering dry, decaying foliage outward from where he stood. I watched and waited, wondering which leaf Calvin would take to be the last leaf, which of the many fallings of leaves would move Calvin to leaf raking.

But before the last leaf came, the first snow fell.

Throughout the neighborhood the snow stood five or six inches high; but in our yard—two feet, white on top the firm foundation of Calvin's decaying, unraked autumn savings.

On the morning of the snowfall, I stood on the front porch surveying our taller yard. When Calvin came out, I knew I wouldn't have to say anything, that his humiliation of having devised a failed system would be sufficient.

"You see?" he asked as he walked proudly onto the porch. "Whether you rake them or not, the snow comes. And once it does, you can't see them anyway. Now the leaves will just decay under the snow, and when spring comes, most of the leaves will be gone all by themselves. Neat, huh?"

One cannot argue against Providence, nor against such inscrutable, organic logic. But one must try.

I explained to Calvin that the leaves decaying beneath the snow would compact and eventually smother the grass, that his method would kill the lawn beneath the trees.

He smiled. "Next to raking," he said, in a deeply resonant and philosophical tone, "the thing I hate most is mowing."

The grass was thin beneath the elm this summer. By next summer it will be entirely gone. Because Calvin has Providence and nature on his side, and he has discovered the secret: there are alternatives to what must be done; and if you can bear the alternatives, you need never rake again.